My CHILD, My DISCIPLE

Pastoral Reflections on Parenting

—— by ——

REVEREND R. D. BERNARD

My Child, My Disciple
Pastoral Reflections on Parenting

iUniverse books may be ordered through booksellers or by contacting:

iUniverse
1663 Liberty Drive
Bloomington, IN 47403
www.iuniverse.com
1-800-Authors (1-800-288-4677)

Because of the dynamic nature of the Internet, any web addresses or links contained in this book may have changed since publication and may no longer be valid. The views expressed in this work are solely those of the author and do not necessarily reflect the views of the publisher, and the publisher hereby disclaims any responsibility for them.

KJV
Scripture quotations from the Holy Bible, King James Version (Authorized Version). First published in 1611. Quoted from the KJV Classic Reference Bible.

NLT
Scripture quotations marked NLT are taken from the Holy Bible, New Living Translation, copyright © 1996, 2004, 2007. Used by permission of Tyndale House Publishers, Inc. Carol Stream, Illinois 60188. All rights reserved. Website

Any people depicted in stock imagery provided by Getty Images are models, and such images are being used for illustrative purposes only. Certain stock imagery © Getty Images.

ISBN: 978-1-5320-7709-8 (sc)
ISBN: 978-1-5320-7710-4 (e)

Library of Congress Control Number: 2019907572

Print information available on the last page.

iUniverse rev. date: 06/28/2019

Table of Contents

MY CHILD, MY DISCIPLE

Pastoral Reflections on Parenting

The late Mr. and Mrs. Lee A. Bernard, Sr. - 1986

"Honor thy father and thy mother." Exodus 20:12 (KJV)

Preface

One of the greatest challenges of this and successive generations is to encourage parents to actively parent their children. All of us who have children and even some of us who have grandchildren, have at some point been disappointed or let down by the choices made by our progeny. We don't need government statistics to convince us of the fact that each successive generation grows more untoward in its attempt at parenting.

Indeed, with each successive generation, we lose more and more of the lost art of parenting. This work is not an attempt to posit myself, my beliefs, or my family as being the gold standard on parenting; it is quite the contrary. I believe all the experts on raising children are no longer with us.

Those of us who are living now may faintly remember someone who knew how to raise children long ago. I would argue that you would have to go a few generations back, to find such people.

This belief does not mean that we were raised by those who did not love us, or that we didn't love them; neither does it mean that they didn't do a decent job in raising us; or even that we didn't do a good job in raising our children. It simply means that we could have done better and there are others who lived before us who did do better. This work is dedicated to them.

Pastoral Reflections on Parenting is both personal and pastoral in nature. Personal in the sense that my wife, Valerie, our two sons, David and Daniel, and I have all shared portions of our lives throughout these pages.

Most of my personal remembrances and recollections are found in very detailed journals that I have kept since July of 1996. Most of my entries are humorous, some are painful, most of them are private, but they are all helpful in understanding parenting – and a few other things as well!

Of a necessity, this work is also pastoral because quite often the failures of yesterday's parenting form the prayers proceeding from the pastor's prayer closet. Hence, my many pastoral observations are grounded in the truth of Scripture as well as in the practicality of being a parent.

Pastoral Reflections on Parenting is a good guide book. Its truths should be introduced as early as possible. Ideally it is for those in their mid-to-late teens who may be considering dating. This is when the good choices that result in effective parenting first become evident.

Pastoral Reflections on Parenting is also a wonderful reference book for those of any age who are attempting to raise children of faith. Most of us will be parents and grandparents longer than we will be anything else in life. It is my prayer that this work will prove helpful in this most important endeavor.

This work focuses on the early years of a child's development and the positive, pervasive impact provided by strong, godly parenting. It is not intended to be comprehensive; rather its purpose is to provide broad guidance and my own "Pastoral Reflections on Parenting."

Section 1– Prelude to Parenting

Reginald D. Bernard – 1986
Lanier High School

"We can make our plans, but the Lord determines our steps." Proverbs 16:9 (NLT)

The word "prelude" is a musical term. It indicates a musical selection or medley of selections that will be played prior to a religious program. A prelude "sets the tone" so to speak. Parents need a spiritual prelude - some teaching to set the tone - before they actually become parents.

It seems to me that more and more Christian parents are surprised by the not-so-Christian actions of their children. Small children are being caught innocently kissing. Others are being caught simulating or actually having "relations."

Prepubescent children can be seen openly practicing the latest sexually suggestive dances. When parents hear of the actions of their children, they seem surprised; but when I hear of them, I am not surprised at all.

What does surprise me is that the parenting skills didn't rise to the level needed to address the situation. Although children have lived around their parents since day one of their lives, parents don't understand that children still have secret lives to which parents are not privy.

Parents don't understand their children as much as they need to, and as much as they think they do. Biblically, this is where we all fall short: we don't understand the secret lives of children – although we have all been children.

Without the guidance and direction of parents, children will secretly (and sometimes not-so-secretly) grow toward whatever is closest to them. Parents must not only parent for what they can see, but also for what they can't. And while parenting books are great, their foundation must be the truth of the Word of God. Those of us who think otherwise enter the role of parenting with a spiritual deficit.

Far from being an ancient code or arcane rulebook, the living and active Word of God shapes the social values and norms of children, creating for them more vibrant and fulfilling lives. The Bible has instruction for every phase of life that any person who is alive will ever encounter.

Once a person surrenders his life to Christ, or rather becomes a Christian, the Bible, the very Word of God, becomes the road map. From the 1st century to the 21st, God's Word remains the standard against which the lives of Christians are to be measured. The psalmist put it this way in Psalm 119:89: *"Forever, O Lord, thy word is settled in heaven."*

The Bible is the lens through which Christians should interpret the world around them. Thus the challenge of parenting is more than met through the sufficiency of the Word of God. Any other parenting instructions, sacred or secular, including *My Child, My Disciple* must be measured based on its faithfulness to the timeless principles of the Word of God.

Now back to the prelude. A prelude to parenting would include dating, an eventual marriage, and ultimately conception and birth within marriage. Now don't put *My Child, My Disciple* away if you failed to get these "preliminaries" in the right order! The world is full of failures and disappointments, but the job of parenting doesn't have to be one of them, even if you skipped the prelude!

Reginald, Valerie Bernard (Pregnant with David)
and Janet Samuel – June 2000

CHAPTER 1 – FIRST THINGS FIRST

Reginald, Valerie, Daniel and David Bernard - 2017

"Therefore if any man be in Christ, he is a new creature: old things are passed away; behold, all things are become new." 2 Corinthians 5:17 (KJV)

"What in the world could God be doing with me?" R. D. Bernard, journal entry May 8, 1997

There is a very basic building block that lies at the foundation of each truly rooted and anchored Christian. That foundation is this: I am not going to allow anything or anybody to come between me and my God. It will not be my mother, my father, my sister, my brother, my lover, my coach, my cousin, my teacher, or my "*self.*"

This basic building block is foundational for living a life of faith. It should be impossible to get so close to a Christian that you come between them and God.

I saw this quality in my wife, Valerie, and she saw this same quality in me - at least that is what she said! God brought our lives together based on this foundational building block. We didn't wait until we got married to let God establish it. This basic building block was already established in our lives before we met over twenty years ago. That is why we knew that certain activities were off limits while we were dating. It didn't have to be said.

We also knew that after we married we would have a strong church life under whose covering and teachings we would raise our children. Valerie and I had strong track records of serving the Lord through His Church.

My wife was 31 years old when we got married and she had never dated anyone in her Church. In fact, nobody was even remotely interested in her – to my knowledge. Perhaps it was because she practiced modesty in how she displayed her femininity. Of course, it could have also been because she didn't engage in spurious conversation with the men or other women of the Church.

These characteristics are part and parcel of possessing this basic building block that God puts in the life of each believer. Paul expressed the same thought this way in 1st Corinthians 2:5: "*That your faith should not stand in the wisdom of men, but in the power of God.*"

The wisdom of men teaches us that we should never be lonely. But my wife went through many lonely nights. I also went through the lonely nights. Our perception of those nights was that it was better to be lonely than disobey God.

Friends, don't wait until you get in a relationship to attempt to build a life. Christians should have a foundational stone on which their lives have already been established prior to dating. If God can't be the head of a Christian, that "Christian" is not qualified for dating or marriage. Each participant in a relationship should already possess this very basic building block.

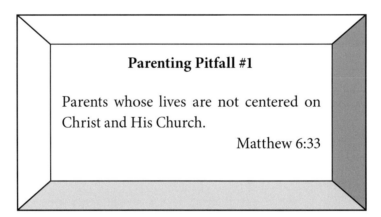

Parenting Pitfall #1

Parents whose lives are not centered on Christ and His Church.

Matthew 6:33

As was mentioned in the Prelude to Parenting, to understand how to raise a child can be rediscovered through the Scriptures. I do understand that there are those who have some specialized training in early childhood education. There have been hundreds of studies in pre-natal and newborn social development.

Yet even amid the most advanced child development theories, each successive generation of children is exposed to increasingly poorer parenting. Just ask any father who is looking for a suitable candidate for his daughter to marry.

He will tell you that a real man of integrity, one who will stick to his word and take care of his daughter, is hard to find. Using the words of Job 1:1, where are the *"perfect and upright men,"* those of *"complete integrity"*? Heck, there are some mature women who want to know the answer to that question!

If you are still not convinced, ask any mother whose son is caught up in *"baby mama drama,"* and she will ask you in the words of Proverbs 31:10, *"Who can find a virtuous woman?"* (NLT) Using the words of Proverbs 31:11, where is the woman that a man can *"trust, and who will greatly enrich his life?"* (NLT)

Where is the woman who, in the words of Proverbs 31:12, *"will not hinder him, but help him all her life"*? (NLT) Again, there are some mature, single men who want to know where these women are!

According to Scripture, men of integrity and women of virtue don't just happen haphazardly or appear out of nowhere. Men of integrity and women of virtue are parented in this manner.

In the words of Proverbs 22:6, they are *"trained up in the way that they should go."* They are also few and far between due to the lost art of parenting.

David and Daniel in 2004 with their paternal
great-grandmother, Antonia Tucker Bernard

KEY DISCIPLE-MAKING POINTS

1. Do you agree that salvation is the basic building block on which a successful life should be built? Why or why not?

_____

_____

_____

2. Do you consider yourself a Christian?

_____

     a.   When were you baptized? _____

             _____

     b.   Are you an active member of the local Church?

             _____

     c.   How often do you participate in the shared life of the Church – outside of worship?

             _____

3. How much emphasis should Christians place on the Word of God as it pertains to dating, marriage, and parenting children?

_____

_____

_____

4. Would you date or marry a person who does not practice strong Christian beliefs? Why or why not?

_____

_____

_____

5. Do you agree that "*men of integrity*" and "*women of virtue*" can be brought forth through active Christian parenting?

_____

_____

_____

CHAPTER 2 – THE PURPOSE OF GODLY DATING

Valerie and Reginald (on a date) – July 3, 1998

"That He might seek a godly seed…" Malachi 2:15

"Today I begin life anew. I accept the wife that is mine by divine right." R. D. Bernard, journal entry July 25, 1996

Those who would not make good parents disqualify themselves by the choices they make when dating. Parenting begins with dating. Not just casual dating, but dating with an eye toward marriage and children. I have told David and Daniel more than once that if I didn't do anything else right, at least I gave them a good mother by my dating choices.

When I met Valerie I noticed how much she adored children. Even in a room full of strangers, she was drawn to the children. She would comment about how cute they were, and how she wished the parents would allow her to hold them.

With her relatives and friends Valerie was even more expressive of her love of children. It stood to reason that she would really love her own. We dated, not only with marriage in mind, but also a view toward children.

One would think that a woman who loved children as much as she does would have wanted more than anything to have children of her own, but that was not so. Valerie hesitated at the thought of having her own children.

She told me more than once, *"children are such a big responsibility."* With regard to my own thoughts about having children, I didn't hesitate. I wanted to have four children; but initially, Valerie didn't want to have any. But perhaps I am getting ahead of myself.

When I wrote the journal entry at the beginning of this chapter, I was in the midst of a bad break-up. Yes, we have all had them. I have had a few! I had broken one of the cardinal rules of Christian dating: a person who is interested in you is not necessarily eligible to date you. Fathers, that is also a good guide for your teen-aged daughters! It is one that I have also shared with my sons.

Christians should only date with a view toward marriage and children. The original mandate was that Adam and Eve would experience the one-flesh union of marriage, and from this union would come godly children.

Good parenting begins with responsible dating. When it comes to Christian dating, only those who are eligible (e.g., saved, celibate, churched, with an eye toward marriage) should apply. Christians don't date recreationally. Christians date those who are eligible – not necessarily those who merely show an interest.

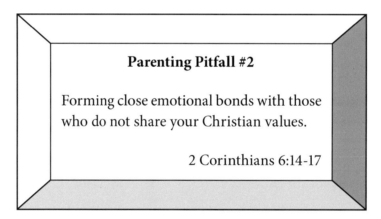

Parenting Pitfall #2

Forming close emotional bonds with those who do not share your Christian values.

2 Corinthians 6:14-17

My prayer was that the Lord would send me a wife and that I would be celibate until He did. I am thankful that I had a busy job that kept me traveling and needed all of my attention. It was not until October of 1997 that I met the lady who was to be my wife "by divine right." I remember it well.

It was another late fall evening – not a particularly busy time on the job. I was home at a reasonable hour, which meant boredom for a single man who was used to traveling and working long hours.

This particular evening I spent praying, sprawled on the floor of my den. I was praying earnestly for a wife. In those days I thought of myself as a chick-magnet – so I had to pray without ceasing!

I had a three bedroom home in a nice neighborhood, a sports car, a professional, well-paying job, and I loved the Lord! That was also a bad combination for *"possessing my vessel in sanctification and honor."* So I prayed *"the more earnestly"* that God would send me a wife and keep me until He did.

As I finished my prayer that evening, I sat up with my back against the sofa and the phone rang. The ringing startled me, as I was still in a state of prayerful meditation. I don't believe in coincidences, so I answered the phone with expectation.

It was one of the ladies from the Church – Mrs. Sarah McCullough. "*Reg-inald,*" she could just stretch out a person's name. "*I have somebody I want you to meet. And look, Reg-inald, she has the same name that you do! I showed her your picture in the paper.*" Sister McCullough was one of those people who would say something, be tickled by what she said, and then laugh loudly at her own statement.

Well, everyone always seems to know someone that they think is a good match for you. But this time it was different. The timing of the call had my request to God fresh on my mind. The fact that the connection was from the Church was also not lost on me.

Mrs. McCullough told me that Valerie Reginal was a 6th grade math teacher and that she was a "nice, Christian lady." Ok, I knew that those were code words for "ugly," but still, I hadn't heard anything that would disqualify her. Soon, perhaps the very next night, Valerie and I were on the phone. She sounded so mature. I couldn't wait to meet her.

We agreed to meet at a restaurant, and when we did, I think we both proceeded with the end in mind. There were no games being played. Shortly after, I met her family and she was introduced to mine.

We were attending one another's church services and after a few months her Pastor was counseling us for marriage. Valerie and I had known one another for only nine months. At seventeen months we were married. That may sound quick to you, but there are some godly principles that guided us both along the way.

Principal #1 – Don't Be Afraid to Cast a Wider Net

The first principle is when you don't get the results that you believe you should have gotten, don't be afraid to cast a wider net. Not everybody in your immediate environs will appreciate the person that you are, the sacrifices that you have made, or even what God is doing in your life. They may not appreciate what you can offer and what you proverbially "*bring to the table.*"

This is why sometimes you need to cast a wider net. If there is nobody in your immediate social circle who is traveling in the same direction that you are; if there is nobody who believes in the saved, sanctified, you; if there are only a few people who can be supportive of what God is doing in this season of your life; then that is a good sign that you need to find some others who are interested in what you are becoming.

Sometimes God can't bless us where we are because we keep trying to work with the same old people who have sent us the same old message: they don't care about us. None of us should be content with neglect, when there are others who will gladly celebrate the godly person that we are becoming.

To not cast a wider net, means to not walk through the door that God has opened for you. That same door may not be open for the people who are presently in your life. In other words, they may not be able to walk through it with you.

I knew that some ladies were off limits for me because I had outgrown certain patterns of life and all the drama that those patterns brought to my life. Valerie had learned as well, that what is tall and good-looking may not have been good for her.

KEY DISCIPLE-MAKING POINTS

1. To date with marriage and parenting in mind, list some situations that you must outgrow.

_____

_____

_____

2. What are some ways that you can cast a wider net?

_____

_____

_____

3. How do the choices we make when we are dating, qualify or disqualify us from being the best parents we can possibly be?

_____

_____

_____

4. How can fear limit us in our desire to please God while we are dating?

_____

_____

5. How does one cast a wider net without looking desperate?

_____

_____

_____

Principal #2 – "Interested" Doesn't Mean "Eligible"

Many are called but few are chosen. Everybody who is interested in you is not eligible to be in your circle. Interest does not mean eligibility. Just because somebody is interested in you doesn't mean that you should automatically allow them into your circle. The experienced fisherman will throw many fish back.

Ladies, you shouldn't keep every phone number that a man gives you. Not every electronic message ought to be answered. Not every look from a man ought to be returned with a look of interest from you. Remember, you are dating with purpose. Not every man is eligible to be your husband or to be the father of your children. Don't waste time with those who are not eligible.

I can remember calling Valerie my *"Tuesday-Thursday"* girlfriend because it seemed we only talked two days per week. If she called and I did not answer, she didn't leave a message and she didn't call back. She also didn't call every day.

I got the sense that she would not allow me to "stalk" her even though I wanted to! I had not yet reached her inner circle. It was too early. She was fine with the few close friends and the life she already had.

As a school teacher, cheer sponsor, Sunday school teacher, choir member, and church finance committee member, her life was already full. She didn't know enough about me to immediately allow me into her inner circle, even though I felt like I was a terrific catch!

Again, to the ladies, a man has to be eligible to enter your circle and the criterion for eligibility has to be something other than looks. It has to be the size of his heart and whether his heart belongs to God.

When you cast a wider net, many are going to show up who are simply not ready. Just because they are interested, it doesn't mean that they are capable of shouldering the responsibility of being a husband and father.

Of course this also means that you should not let a man address you any kind of way – even if you are only dating. Furthermore, just because he was there when nobody else was there, or perhaps he did that one favor for you, still does not mean that he is the one for you.

Likewise, men, the experienced hunter wants to go where there is a lot of game, but that doesn't mean that he is going to shoot everything he sees. Much of what he sees, he will let pass because that is not what he is looking for. Not every woman is fit to be the mother of your child.

Friends, draw a big crowd into your life, but that doesn't mean that everybody gets to come to your inner circle or that they should even know where you live. Go out and enjoy the world.

Meet as many Christians as you can, but that doesn't mean that all of them will make it to your inner circle. Not everyone should be invited to your home or even know your number. You may know a lot of people, but only a few should be allowed to get close to you.

KEY DISCIPLE-MAKING POINTS

1. List the requirements that you have for someone of the opposite sex to parent your child.

   _____

   _____

   _____

2. Name some that you have eliminated who were interested, but who were also not eligible.

   _____

   _____

   _____

3. Would you sacrifice your standards/requirements for a person who does not meet them and who is not interested in even changing to meet them?

   _____

   _____

   _____

4. What effect do you think your standards/dating requirements will have on any future children you may have?

   _____

   _____

   _____

5. If you already have children, what effect did your dating standards/requirements have on your children (i.e. what type of relationship do they have with their other parent)?

   _____

   _____

   _____

Daniel and David – 2004

Principal #3 – Refuse Leftovers

If we do not approach relationships from the pattern that God has set forth in Scripture, when we show up at the table, there will only be leftovers. If you ever want to be successful in love, you must bring something to the table besides leftovers.

Leftovers may work for the young, ill-informed and ill-advised. Leftovers may even work to catch an old fool, but for the woman or man of God, leftovers, as it pertains to the opposite sex, are never enough – especially when assessing parenting potential.

Young ladies, a man will never see you, the you of you, who you really are in your heart, if you are serving leftovers. Young men, most ladies are intimidated by a man who cannot be manipulated sexually. You can quickly determine who is not eligible.

Now I am not one to turn my back on leftovers, and I can make a good meal out of scraps, but what I refuse to do, is to take leftovers from somebody else's house and make them my main course. From the moment I met Valerie, I knew that she was nobody's leftover. (I just didn't know what she saw in me!)

God has declared that men and women should come together in marriage, not because they are madly in love and wildly romantic; rather, because somebody named Jesus brought them together.

In a first century Jewish betrothal or engagement, the couple barely knew one another. They were both assumed to be virgins, they both came from two-parent homes, and they both were members of the synagogue.

I know from experience that this combination works. Christian couples should be at the same speed sexually – both novices not having known the act of sex. They should be the same or similar from a family perspective, in that they both come from families who are under covenant with God. Any other way, is to bring leftovers to what should be a marriage feast.

How you date is how you will marry. If it was sex, or sex appeal that caught you, it will take sex or sex appeal to keep you. Sex without God will ultimately kill your relationship and destroy any chance you have at healthy parenting. Christian men have to look past a woman's sex appeal to see her heart. Is God in her heart?

When I first laid eyes on Valerie, she looked like a mother. Her maturity, calm demeanor, and quiet spirit all spoke volumes to me. This was a woman who would make an excellent mother. I did not understand why she was not already "taken." Of course, I looked for things that would disqualify her, but I found none.

During those days, I asked my soon-to-be fiancée how she felt about children. She replied that children were such a responsibility that she didn't care to have any. She in turn asked me my thoughts. I told her that I thought she was right. A great portion of a person's independence and their "*right to be selfish*" in their own homes and with their own lives should end with the birth of a child.

Although I was not in ministry at the time, I explained to her that I felt that if we were married, it would be our Christian responsibility, if we had children, to raise them to honor God.

At the time, I distinctly remembered the words of Psalm 127:4, the portion that reads: "*Children born to a young man are like sharp arrows in a warrior's hands.*" (NLT)

Valerie asked me how many children did I see myself having, if any. I told her, "*four,*" and she answered, "*What about two?*" The rest is history. I don't know what most twenty-seven-year-old men look for, but what I was looking for was someone who would make an excellent wife and mother.

Sadly, many men never get past the level of leftovers and table scraps when God has promised His people a great feast. Why are so many content to feast on leftovers?

Young ladies, present yourself to a man in a manner that will help him see your heart. A real man, a godly man, will require you to win his mind before he hands over his heart.

He will not settle for leftovers or table scraps that he can get anywhere. If a man says he is godly, and yet he wants to make you a leftover, and you really want to be with him, then train him to love your heart by saying "no," and refusing to become his leftover.

By the time you allow a man to kiss you, he should know all of your family, they should know him, and there should be a ring on your finger. This way, you both bring something other than leftovers to the marriage feast.

KEY DISCIPLE-MAKING POINTS

1. Do your dating patterns indicate that you are dating with marriage in mind? Why or why not?

_____

_____

_____

2. How do you keep someone's sex appeal from blurring their potential as a parent?

_____

_____

_____

3. Do you dress to emphasize your sex-appeal or your potential as a parent?

_____

_____

_____

4. How similar is your background to that of the person you are dating?

_____

_____

_____

5. Are your core values (e.g. God, Church, work, dating, money, marriage, children) the same or similar as those of the person you are dating?

_____

_____

_____

Daniel and David - 2004

Principal #4 – Blended Families - "Extra-Care Required"

When dating someone who already has at least one child, extra care is required. Some of the most spiritually beautiful, God-honoring people already have children. Their status as parents should not disqualify them should God choose to bring them into your life. However, extra-care is required when assessing their eligibility to become a part of your life.

Valerie is such a good mother that I am sure that if she already had children when we met, her love for them would have only drawn me closer to her. Men, ladies who are already parents should have readily visible parenting skills.

Time is needed to assess whether the stage of life this person is in, along with their experiences with the child's other biological parent, will fit into where you believe God is leading you as a parent or potential parent.

Children who are already being raised are being raised under a set of values – whether stated or unstated. When dating a person who is already a parent, do you share the values under which she is raising her child?

It is a bit more complex for ladies who date men who are already fathers. Since men are usually non-custodial parents, ladies cannot readily observe their parenting values.

Ladies, you will only know what he tells you. You should seek to understand the dynamics of his past relationship (e.g. was he married, how did it end, was the pregnancy planned, does he pay child support). How has this man's past relationships qualified him to be the leader of your family and your child's father? Is this person stable enough to build a life around?

Our lives are building projects. They must be built on the foundation of Jesus Christ (1st Corinthians 3:11). We are the builders on this foundation (1st Corinthians 3:10-15). God is building a life for you – using you and your spouse as building blocks around which other blocks will be added.

Everything in your life is attached to you in some way. That is precisely why your life is called "your" life. God is busy building around you. To use a sports metaphor, you are the franchise. As the basic building block in your life, if you are unstable, then what God is attempting to build will also be unstable. A structure is only as stable or sturdy as the material of which it is made.

If marriage is in your plans, your union with your spouse then becomes the basic building block. God then builds your life around your marriage. Marriages are either stable or unstable because those who are in the marriage are stable or unstable. Some marriages fall apart totally because the builders walked away – one or both of them were too unstable. The likelihood of this type of failure increases with blended families.

This is why extra care is required. The lives of children, step-children, and grandchildren can be unstable, because their parents, step-parents, and grandparents, the builders, didn't provide the stability. In these cases, it becomes critical that the lives of those seeking to be married and start a new family be firmly rooted in the most stable of institutions – the Church.

David – July 2005

KEY DISCIPLE-MAKING POINTS

1. Do you see evidence of the best and highest values of your potential spouse in his or her child?

   _____

   _____

   _____

2. Would you accept the job of parenting that your potential spouse has already done with regard to any future children you may have together?

   _____

   _____

   _____

3. How stable is your potential spouse's relationship with the Church? (e.g. How long has he or she been a member, how do they serve, what lasting spiritual relationships have they formed)

   _____

   _____

   _____

4. What type of relationship does your potential spouse have with his or her child's other parent?

   _____

   _____

   _____

5. Will you be allowed to fully parent any potential step-children?

   _____

   _____

   _____

Chapter 3 – A Christian Marriage

Reginald and Valerie Bernard – February 27, 1999

"For this cause shall a man leave his father and mother, and shall be joined unto his wife, and they two shall be one flesh. This is a great mystery: but I speak concerning Christ and the Church."
Ephesians 5:31-32 (KJV)

Valerie and I were married on Saturday, February 27, 1999 at 4:00 pm in the afternoon. It rained hard that afternoon. Thank God that the old wives' tale about stormy wedding days being a good predictor of bad marriages is not true! The Mt. Charity Baptist Church of Ridgeland, Mississippi, Valerie's childhood church and now my church, was packed that stormy afternoon in February. That was the wedding.

Valerie and I were more interested in the marriage. We left the Church after dark and were chauffeured by family friend James Stewart, of Peoples Funeral Home, to suite 1001 of the Hilton Hotel on East County Line Road in Jackson, Mississippi. The next morning, we left for our honeymoon and the rest of our lives.

In many ways we were just like any other newly married couple – so happy to be together and yet trying to get accustomed to it all! From the very beginning there was no birth control. I laughed to myself when I thought of the very first question that was asked of me in pre-marital counseling: *"Did I like women?"* Of course, I did!

In marriage, I could lawfully enjoy one! Valerie and I had a very frank discussion about children prior to our wedding: she didn't want any at all because of the responsibility; I wanted four, so we agreed on two.

I also ended up changing jobs in the summer of 1998 so that I would not be away from home after hours. Our plan was to live on one salary – mine.

This change in employers was a part of the larger moves that we were both making in preparation for our life together. Valerie continued her work in the public-school system with the expectation that she would be a stay-at-home mother as soon as God said so.

After we decided that we would have two children, we needed to choose a church to attend. She had only been a member of one church her whole life; so had I. We both knew from Scripture that it was her responsibility to follow her husband.

Her pastor and one of the deacons at her church told her that they would miss her, but that she would always have their prayers. They fully expected her to leave. After all, she was marrying a saved man who would be devoted to her. In their way of thinking, she should follow him to his church.

But this is not what we did. Our commitment to our future children, even though we were not yet married, caused me to leave my church one month before we were married and join her church. We both agreed that her church did a much better job of training children.

My church had very few children. It had very little in the way of structured, organized teaching. The people there were sincere, but it was not enough of them to have an organized youth ministry. Yes, my wife and I could have dedicated ourselves to building one; and that was what many people expected us to do.

But why build one, when her church already had one with children growing up through it? She had a Pastor who took the time to dedicate children during morning worship. My pastor didn't, because we didn't have enough children being born.

Through many tears, I had to leave the only church I had ever known. That was also my parent's church. I had to make that sacrifice. If I did not, my wife and I would not have put our children in the position to receive the best religious instruction.

The "*train*" in "*train up a child*" includes an organized church program. Young children **need** to be in church. Too many in our day are attempting to raise children of faith without the help of the house of God or without a formalized, religious training program.

We looked at each of our churches, and decided that hers, the Mt. Charity Baptist Church, had the most to offer a family. The clincher was the time and effort Pastor B. L. Ervin put into our pre-martial sessions. I joined there in January of 1999.

The first few months of our marriage was one big honeymoon. The congratulatory calls and cards just kept coming! It seemed as if everyone who knew me was telling her, "*you have found yourself a good husband;*" and everyone who knew her was telling me, "*you have found yourself a good wife.*"

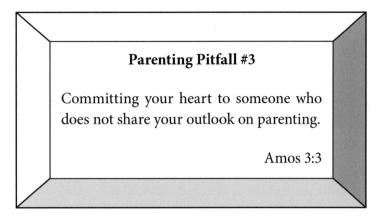

Parenting Pitfall #3

Committing your heart to someone who does not share your outlook on parenting.

Amos 3:3

We were simply content with one another; but I was not content with my "bachelor pad." In my mind it was much too small to accommodate a wife, and prayerfully, two children. Additionally, I didn't want Valerie to think she was moving into "my" home. I wanted the home in which we raised our children to be "our" home – not just "my" home.

Within eight months we made an offer on a much larger home, which in my mind, was more accommodating to family life and a sense of one-ness. Valerie didn't seem to care where we lived, as long as we were together.

Our timing was fortuitous because in that ninth month of marriage, November 1999, we became pregnant! In fact, we celebrated Thanksgiving, the pregnancy, and our new home over the same weekend.

Gosh, there were boxes that still needed to be unpacked and thank-you notes that were not yet written!

David and Daniel – June 2007

KEY DISCIPLE-MAKING POINTS

1. When marriage is imminent, what are some of the more critical decisions that need to be made as it pertains to raising children of faith?

   _____

   _____

   _____

2. Are some occupations more suitable to family life and the raising of children than others?

   _____

   _____

   _____

3. In your opinion, what is an ideal home and neighborhood for raising children of faith?

   _____

   _____

   _____

   a. Should this ideal be incorporated in the marriage plans? Why or why not?

      _____

   b. Should the home and the Church be closely knit in the raising of children of faith? Why or why not?

      _____

      _____

4. Are both of you willing to sit down with a pastor, long before a wedding, for pre-marital sessions?

   _____

   _____

   _____

5. Why is it especially important that the home be considered a "neutral" site (i.e., not belonging to either party in the marriage prior to marriage)?

   _____

   _____

   _____

Section 2 – So You're Pregnant!

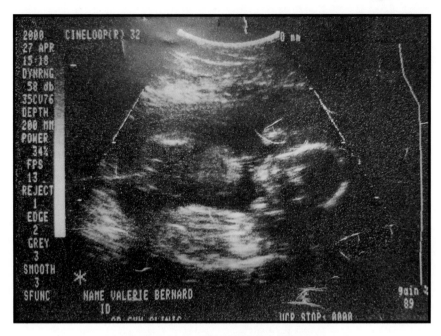

Sonogram image of David Reginald Bernard

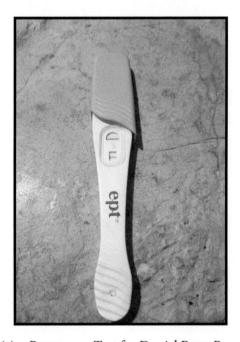

Positive Pregnancy Test for Daniel Ryan Bernard

"As arrows are in the hand of a mighty man; so are children of the youth." Psalm 127:4 (KJV)

When Valerie took a home pregnancy test and it gave a positive result, our lives became a mixture of emotions. We had just purchased a new home. We were not in it thirty days before we found out that we were going to be parents! I can still remember the prayer of dedication in our new home when I prayed for the children that I hoped would live there. Our lives in that home were for them.

With the good news came a wave of emotion and thoughts about parenthood – mostly about our own parents and the events surrounding our own births. Even though this pregnancy was lovingly planned, Valerie and I both wondered whether we were really qualified.

After all, we had been married for less than a year and had just purchased a new home. What qualified us to be parents? Sure, we took care of the "Prelude to Parenting;" we dated with the intention of being married, and yes, we ultimately married. Now this!

Just in case you have skipped the Prelude to Parenting of Section 1, maybe you didn't date with the intention of marrying, and perhaps you didn't get married before a child was conceived.

The good news is that you are still in time for the main attraction - which is the birth and parenting of your child – so there is hope. Just like the previews at the movies, even some Christian parents don't pay attention to the "Prelude to Parenting." To you, I say that God, in His sovereignty, has still seen fit to allow the miracle of creation and childbirth to enter your life. You are now changed forever!

The record in Heaven will reflect that, among other things, you are now a parent as well. Whether you were married when you conceived or not; whether you love the person with whom you created this life or not; or whether you think you are old enough, financially stable enough, or not, is now irrelevant. A child is on the way and you are just in time for one of the most important parts of parenting, which is the beginning.

The Bernards on Swan Lake

Chapter 4 – Conception to Birth

Valerie (pregnant with David), Brenda Bernard and Alfreda Bernard Jackson – June 2000

"I will praise thee; for I am fearfully and wonderfully made: marvelous are thy works; and that my soul knoweth right well." Psalm 139:14 (KJV)

"Today, I found out that I am going to be a Daddy – again. I am not really nervous like I was with David. I just wish my income were more stable and that I liked my job." R. D. Bernard, journal entry – January 16, 2002

Have you ever given thought to what your mother and father were like when you were born? Have you ever imagined what their relationship was like? Do you know how they met? Did they love one another? Were they married? Who chose your name?

Somehow when we try to place our parents in the past, we endow them with magical qualities. We believe the best about our parents because they are our first heroes. This "hero-worship" causes us to see them in a light that is not altogether healthy.

Children hate to hear that their parents had to "relate" for them to get here. I still cringe to think about it! We all want to believe that we are the special product of a man and a woman who genuinely loved one another. Of course, this is the way that the Word of God designs it.

It all begins with a godly man - like Adam in Genesis 2:8. God will then bring him a wife who loves God but who loves him as well – like Eve in Genesis 2:18. The two of them refrain from "relations" until they are married. Once they are married, they will bring God glory as a one-flesh union, much like Adam and Eve did in Genesis 2:23-24.

Now a part of the glory of marriage is the creation of sons and daughters. You may remember that Adam and Eve were commanded to "*be fruitful and multiply.*" Then they, their offspring, and God Himself, would all live happily ever after.

In the day and age in which we live, this is just not so. From the moment we are conceived; the moment that we become a fertilized egg in our mother's uterus, we begin to participate in a world of sin.

Quite often mother and father didn't know each other that well at all. Some of us are the products of proms and others of us are the products of other one-night stands. Some of us may have had our paternity called into question.

We know who mother is, but we may not know who father is. We know what we were told, but we have come to find out that we were conceived in the midst of a love triangle, or maybe even a love "quadrilateral." Sadly, it happens.

Let's strip away the fairy tale language. Just for a moment, consider the fact that mother and father were ordinary men and women just like us. They had desires like us. They made bad choices just like we do. They drank. They partied. They courted: just like we do. They also had disagreements.

As small, small children, we were right there in the midst of their lives, even though we may not consciously remember it. Did you know that babies can hear and recognize voices even while they are still in the womb?

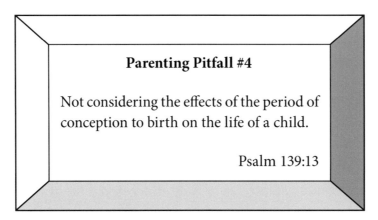

Parenting Pitfall #4

Not considering the effects of the period of conception to birth on the life of a child.

Psalm 139:13

How many male voices did we hear while we were still in the womb? Were they friendly voices? Were they aggressive voices? Did they speak lovingly to our mothers? Was mother's voice calm and reassuring, or was it nervous and jittery?

How much music did we hear? Was it the kind that stimulates mental development or the type that retards mental development? Valerie and I prayed with each of our children before they were born – nightly, within their hearing. I even recited the ABC's in hopes of having a young Einstein!

Valerie went even further. She carried on full-length conversations with David and Daniel during the times of their respective pregnancies. As a toddler, David saw it so often with the unborn Daniel that he wanted to "*talk to the baby*" too!

Tone is very important to an unborn child. Tones in the presence of a pregnant woman should be loving and gentle. Babies don't understand language yet, but they do know the sound of their mother's voice and whether her voice and other voices are loving and gentle. Our tones are one way we can communicate love to our children before they are born.

What else do children hear while they are in the womb? They hear everything! How much indecision was there surrounding our birth? Was there any talk around our children about ending their pregnancy in abortion? If so, who was pressuring whom?

For us, all these things happened years ago while we were still in the womb. Today, we are now parents or potential parents. Those events influenced us. The events around our conception and prior to our birth, form the framework and the key to our later lives.

Some people are peaceful in their relationships because there was peace around their conception. Others of us are war-like and hostile. This is due to what we heard from the moment we were conceived.

Did the events surrounding our conception influence us? Sure they did. We just don't realize the extent. Much of what we go through as adults is due, in part, to what we experienced in and around our conception and shortly after we were born.

Pregnancy brings stress into everybody's life. Even though ours was a planned pregnancy, it still brought a fair amount of stress. A mother's thoughts may run something like this – especially with the first pregnancy:

How am I going to take care of this baby? Who is going to pay for this baby being born? Do I really love the father? Should we get married? Should I stop seeing (insert his name here) now that I am pregnant by (insert the father's name here)? What am I going to do about school? What about my job? This is very real stress.

There is also stress on the father. His thoughts may run something like this: *If I am not married to her, is this baby mine? Do I want to marry this woman? If I am seeing somebody else, how is this going to look? Is she going to insist on child support?*

My thoughts, years ago, were very naïve. I just assumed that if I made enough money and provided enough security, then everything would be just fine. *After all,* I reasoned, *this child is going to have more than I ever had.* But on the day that David was born, I was a total wreck. I saw all of the medical intubation that Valerie had to endure.

To complicate matters, we were informed that David had gotten active in the womb when we checked-in the day before. It seems that he felt his mother's stress level increase. When Valerie was given something for her stress, David stopped moving in the womb.

There was concern, briefly, that he had stopped breathing. He too, had to be monitored very closely. In fact, the doctors placed a small object, almost like a screw, into the very top of his head to monitor his vital signs.

When I saw that, I started walking and praying. Not only was my wife stressed, my son was stressed too! After Valerie was medicated and speaking more liberally, I can remember her saying to her mother, "*All that man does is pray.*"

Yes, I prayed every time I felt nervousness coming on. I had asked everyone to join hands more than a few times on the morning of August 31, 2000. My mother-in-law, my brother-in-law Daryl, and my wife's best friend, Brenda, were all cramped into a delivery suite – waiting on the arrival of David Reginald Bernard.

At the time I did not realize that grandparents endure a level of stress as well. I don't know what my mother-in-law thought at the time, but I am sure she was praying too. Perhaps even more stressful are the thoughts of those grandmothers whose grandchildren are being brought into the world in less than ideal circumstances.

A grandmother's thoughts may run something like this: *I know I am going to have to take care of this baby. My daughter is not ready for a child. I hope she doesn't marry the father but she does need to put him on child support. I hope she doesn't drop out of school because of this baby. Maybe I will have to work longer to help out.*

Pregnancies bring a lot of stress. If stressful thoughts were dots, we would all have been born polka-dot babies. Unfortunately, all these thoughts and events do have an effect on children. Children are born, not only looking physically like their parents, but as the spiritual embodiment of all that was surrounding their relationship when they conceived.

It is no wonder that some of us have low self-esteem or are full of anger. Others of us are confused half the time. From the moment we were conceived, we were brought into a world of chaos.

Now fast forward. Think about how it must be with the birth of your child. Whether your child was born this past year or is several years old, think about the level of chaos around his or her conception.

KEY DISCIPLE-MAKING POINTS

1. A healthy, well-adjusted child is the product of a healthy well-adjusted pregnancy. What are (were) the strengths of your child's conception and gestation period?

_____

_____

_____

2. A healthy, well-adjusted child is the product of a healthy well-adjusted pregnancy. What are (were) the weaknesses of your child's conception and gestation period?

_____

_____

_____

3. Is your tone of voice generally loud or soft?

_____

_____

_____

4. What does your tone communicate to your child?

_____

_____

_____

5. Who are the other significant personalities who may have had, or will have, an impact on your child before his or her birth?

_____

_____

_____

Chapter 5 – A Real, Live Birth!

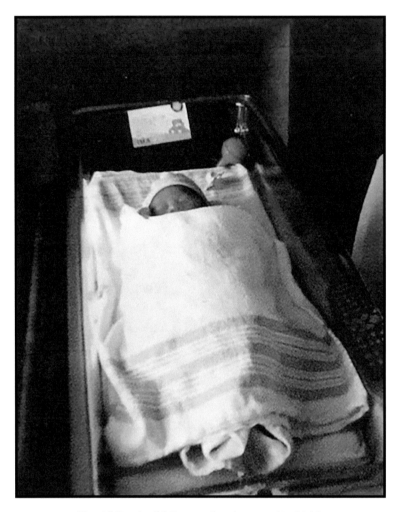

David Reginald Bernard – August 31, 2000

"Children are a gift from the Lord; they are a reward from Him."
Psalm 127:3 (NLT)

I videotaped the births of my two children. I set the camera on a tripod in the corner of the delivery suite and just hit record. I wanted to capture every emotion and all the comings and goings from our suite. The first time Valerie and I looked back at the recordings, we were surprised to not see David or Daniel. In fact, their absence was conspicuous.

Although we knew that there was a time when we didn't have children, they have been with us for so long and we had them so early in marriage that it was hard to remember a time when it was just Valerie and me. It seemed like we went from two people who were just interested in one another, to two people married with two small children.

It is odd what the mind remembers most after so many years. David Reginald Bernard was born on a Thursday at 12:37 in the afternoon. Valerie and I spent two nights at the hospital. David cried so much Thursday night that the nursing staff took him, so we could get some rest.

I can vividly remember being surprised that the hospital was going to let us take David home on Saturday. *Couldn't they let us stay for a few more days?* We didn't master breast-feeding like we had planned, and both mother and child seemed to be upset about it.

In my way of thinking, David didn't seem large enough to be moved from the hospital via private vehicle to our home. *Couldn't they drive us home in an ambulance with a nurse?* I didn't trust driving my family home in my rough-riding sport utility vehicle.

Certainly a life that small and fragile could not be entrusted to us! Although we had planned for this new life, the reality was nearly overwhelming! *Two* of us went to the hospital, but *three* of us were now being asked to leave!

From the first time we laid eyes on David in a sonogram, and especially when we were introduced via his birth, we have loved him. But as the excitement and novelty of childbirth began to wear off and the weariness set in, we just needed David to stop crying long enough for us to take a nap. We didn't realize there would be days when even taking a shower would be difficult.

Although we had a nursery set up at home, we were simply not prepared for the level of responsibility in caring for a newborn. We had read all the best parenting books and studied up on the latest parenting trends and techniques. Now we just had to execute.

There is nothing like a newborn to show you how selfish you really are! Valerie and I quickly abandoned David's crib in his nursery, in favor of him being in our bedroom and even our bed. We just had to get some sleep! When Daniel came along, we didn't buy another crib, we just bought an even bigger bed!

We swore that no one told us parenting newborns would be like that! Our lives literally revolved around David and Daniel. I took time off from work. Valerie left work permanently as we had planned. Valerie also started calling me "*Daddy*" and insisted that I call her "*Mommy.*"

Of course, this was to train David and Daniel. It would be nearly a dozen years before I called my wife anything other than "*Mommy*" in our home, and sometimes we still slip and call one another "*Mommy*" or "*Daddy.*"

We also could no longer raise our voices – not in sudden excitement, and definitely not in anger. We spoke in moderate to low tones with soothing pitches. This was the same way Valerie had trained me to talk to David when he was still in the womb.

The ride home from the hospital was one of the longest rides I have ever had. I am usually a very fast driver, but now I had to drive *below* the speed limit because in Valerie's words, "*we are carrying precious cargo.*" My wife also began her longstanding tradition of riding on the backseat with the baby boys. I was now driving Miss Daisy and her two boys!

When we got home we were greeted with our first sense of security: my mother-in-law. This was the one lady who knew how to raise children. As I got the news that she was coming to live with us "*for a spell,*"

I silently thanked the God of Heaven. She was with us for David, and she also joined us 25 months later for Daniel.

There is no substitute for godly experience. Although I believe our two children are special (as all parents should believe about their kids), there is nothing unique about how to raise them.

Christian parents have been raising godly children for centuries. Even with newborns, there is guidance. One of the most important things to note is that children are "born-into" families.

These families have pre-existing routines (how they do things), and pre-existing relationships (how they interact with each other). These routines and relationships have to be especially tailored for children, particularly new-borns.

The very first emotional impression that a child should have is that of belonging to a loving, secure family unit. In this family unit, each member retains the roles assigned to them by God.

From this Biblical picture, the child learns first how to function as a boy or girl; he or she also learns submission to authority; healthy love (because he or she sees it demonstrated) and develops a strong sense of personhood (because he or she is allowed to grow up safe in the home of both parents). This is disciple-making 101 and it begins with the mother.

A child's first teacher is his or her mother. We all know about the biological connection between a mother and a child; but there is also a spiritual connection.

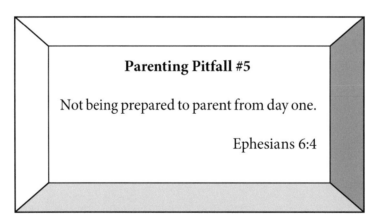

Parenting Pitfall #5

Not being prepared to parent from day one.

Ephesians 6:4

Scripturally speaking, a mother is tasked by God as being the first teacher of the Faith to her child. The Word of God ties mother and child into a spiritually symbiotic relationship. The salvation or belief system of mothers is reflected in their children.

Paul put it this way in 1st Timothy 2:15 in the NLT: "*Women will be saved through childbearing, assuming they continue to live in faith, love, holiness, and modesty.*"

The idea that Paul expresses in this verse is not what it initially sounds like. The plain reading of this verse makes it sound like a woman is saved simply because she has children.

The context and wording in New Testament Greek; however, indicates a much different meaning. A woman's salvation is tied to her role in the family as a mother who raises godly children.

Women should embrace this role! She is the womb that brings forth children; and even after birth, her progeny are still attached to her.

It is this Pastor's observation that the emotional lives of children are passed down, not through father, but through mother. We are who we are by *temperament,* because of our relationship with our mothers.

Whether a person is generally happy, generally sad, or generally crazy is because of mother. The mother's emotional stability and attitude toward the newborn is everything. After all, it is the mother who nourished the child in the womb.

If the mother is bitter (perhaps the father didn't hang around to assume his responsibility); resentful (perhaps she sees the newborn as an interruption of her social life); or unloving (maybe she was not loved properly by her mother) during the pregnancy and early years of that child's spiritual formation; it will be reflected in the life of that child.

The feelings of abandonment and neglect, even in children from so-called "good-homes," are reflective of the mother's emotional stability and attitude toward the newborn.

Mothers who are happy in their God-ordained roles generally have happier, healthier children. Even a single mother can make the best of things by her attitude. A single mother's universe ought to center around disciple-making with regard to her children.

God has given mothers, the cradle of life, a great task in raising and teaching godly children. Again, look at the role that women played in the life of Timothy. 2nd Timothy 1:5 reads in the NLT, "*I know that you sincerely trust the Lord, for you have the faith of your mother, Eunice, and your grandmother, Lois.*" Single mothers, it can be done if you take disciple-making seriously.

1st Timothy 2:15 does not read that "*women will be saved through the pursuit of a father for their child.*"

You will fail in your task of disciple-making if you start bringing "uncles" around your child. You will also fail if you put a man to whom you are not married (and usually not even engaged) before your child. Your child needs your acceptance.

Every child should know the loving, receptive nature of a Mother. Children learn acceptance and love from their mothers. They should be well aware of the pleasing sound of their mother's voice and the soft touch of her skin.

That's right, we learn relational intimacy from our mothers. I can still hear and remember many of the songs Valerie made up and sang to David and Daniel.

There was a song for bath-time. There was a song for meal-time, and a song for bed-time. The songs didn't make sense to me, but she enjoyed singing to them and the babies were enraptured by them. None of us watched television in those days. Mommy and her soft, tender voice was our entertainment!

KEY DISCIPLE-MAKING POINTS

1. Emotionally speaking, are you most like your father or your mother? Explain your answer below.

_____

_____

_____

2. List some ways that mothers demonstrate unconditional love and acceptance to new-borns.

_____

_____

_____

3. Is it possible for a mother to emotionally reject a child? Why or why not?

_____

_____

_____

4. If a child is emotionally rejected, will that rejection be evident later in life? Why or why not?

_____

_____

_____

5. In a blended family, what difficulties may be present in showing unconditional love and acceptance to a newborn?

_____

_____

_____

Section 3 – Proactive Parenting, The Early Years

David – about 15 months

Daniel – about 15 months

"Suffer little children, and forbid them not, to come unto me: for of such is the kingdom of heaven." Matthew 19:14 (KJV)

A mother is sobbing. She is standing outside, near where her adolescent son was murdered. She is crying out *"My baby! My baby!"* The news cameras come and her sadness turns to rage as she shouts into the cameras that her son *"never did anything to anybody!"*

What this mother doesn't realize is that she lost her baby a long, long time ago. He may have been killed on a particular day, but he was lost to her long before then.

Without active parenting, children are spiritually and emotionally lost. We have all witnessed this "lostness" in the lack of general respect and decorum exhibited in some children. Many teenagers refuse to submit in the face of age and wisdom. More than a few even take their way by violence and force.

These situations exist because parents have failed in their most basic task: parenting. Our society is filled with young adults who really are lost children. They have no sense of commitment; no sense of family; indeed, no sense of belonging. Each child that is not actively parented further erodes our collective sense of community.

The penalty for not actively parenting a child is severe. The best way to avoid the penalty is to begin parenting on day one.

Daniel – 2004

CHAPTER 6 – LET THE TRAINING BEGIN!

Daniel and David – October 2003

David – about 10 months

"Train up a child in the way he should go: and when he is old, he will not depart from it." Proverbs 22:6 (KJV)

Early on, Valerie established a routine for David. Feedings began at 6:00 am and every two hours afterwards. When David napped, so did Valerie. When he was awake, they interacted almost constantly. In fact, David began to make "cooing" sounds almost from birth.

After a few months, he was a regular chatterbox. Although we couldn't understand a word of it, we carried on as if we did. I was usually home by the 6 pm feeding, which was followed by bath time. By 8, we were all asleep – at least for a couple of hours.

Parents are responsible for teaching children how to crave order and routine. In a home with young children, there is no such thing as waking up every morning and then trying to plan meals and figure out the activities for that day. Effective parenting must be proactive.

When parents have not established an order or a routine, children will run the home. From the time newborns are brought home from the hospital, to the time they leave the home as adults, there should be some sense of routine. Order and routine are the bedrocks of effective teaching.

The Hebrew word for "*teach*" as it is used in Deuteronomy 6:7 is "*la-mad*" and it means to "*goad.*" A goad is a "*spiked-stick,*" a rod with a pointed end. Symbolically speaking, parents are called to "goad" their children forward in life. This "painful push" is required to introduce children to the routine or the way of life that God has set aside for them. Think of it as one of the earliest forms of structure and order.

The early years are all about structure. Structure, order, and routine are essential for the psychological health of children. A regular schedule assures and promotes the psychological health of children. This is the job of the early home and especially that of the mother, as the child's first teacher.

The parents of newborns and toddlers are charged with creating environments that are regular and predictable. God created us to crave this order. Our minds work best with order. We learn best with order. Homes become more efficient with order.

When there is no structure, order, or routine, the health of children is at risk. Children experience feelings of safety, security, and trust where there is order. Children produced by homes without order are usually emotional train wrecks.

There are three types of homes where it may be challenging to establish and maintain order. These three merit special consideration.

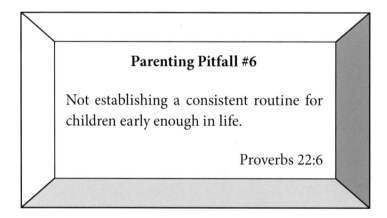

Parenting Pitfall #6

Not establishing a consistent routine for children early enough in life.

Proverbs 22:6

The Single Parent Home

Unless a single parent is independently wealthy, he or she does not have the time to significantly invest in parenting while also earning a decent living. One parent can't provide the level of parenting and psychological preparedness in children that two parents can.

For example, years ago when the boys were younger, Valerie would tell me that she loved the boys so much that they could make it without their father (me)! This is one of the subtle messages our society teaches women of all ages. It is the "*diva mentality*," or the "*I can do the job of two parents*" mentality.

Some successful, well-adjusted, children are the products of single-parent homes. But that doesn't mean that this is the right or even best way to parent children. Unless a single parent can split into two different people who are willing to parent, a single parent home cannot provide the same level of parenting as a two-parent home.

Now some twenty years later, my wife tells me that she and the boys never would have made it to who *they* are with just *her* parenting. Studies have shown that married people make more money, make more plans, and are sometimes healthier psychologically than their single counterparts. Children thrive in the structure, order and routine that can be afforded by a two-parent home.

KEY DISCIPLE-MAKING POINTS

1. What are some ways that single parents can create structured environments for their children?

   _____

   _____

   _____

2. Should small children be exposed to those whom their single parents are dating? Why or why not?

   _____

   _____

   _____

   a. Is this healthy for the children? Explain your answer below.

   _____

   _____

   _____

   b. What might this behavior teach small children?

   _____

   _____

   _____

3. What are some of the financial considerations that must be made by a single parent with small children?

   _____

_____

_____

4. What are some of the social considerations that must be made by a single parent with small children?

_____

_____

_____

5. How should parents ensure that their children are in well-structured environments when they are away from their parents?

_____

_____

_____

Valerie and David – Christmas 2000

The Home Affected by Divorce

The second type of home where it may be challenging to establish and maintain order is the home that has been affected by divorce. Over the years, there have been dozens of studies on divorce and very few of them have found anything good that comes from it.

In fact, divorce has been shown to diminish a child's future competence in many areas of life including: family relationships, education, emotional well-being, and future earning power.

After a divorce, parents don't have as much time and emotional strength to invest in parenting. Likewise, the children of divorced parents will likely attempt to spend the most time with the parent who sets fewer boundaries. This is why children can't be trusted to make decisions about their futures. Parents must make these decisions.

Psychologically, parents who have suffered the trauma of divorce need time to heal and rediscover themselves. While parents are traveling through this emotional "no-man's land," the children suffer. A lack of parental focus leads to unstructured environments.

KEY DISCIPLE-MAKING POINTS

1. What are some ways that divorcees' can create structured environments for their children?

2. Name some specific child considerations for parents who are considering divorce.

3. What are some ways that parents who are divorced can work together to create structured, orderly environments in both homes?

4. What other parenting resources may be available to parents who need assistance with parenting while going through a divorce?

5. What are some proactive steps that parents who are divorcing can take to reduce the disruption to children?

_____

_____

_____

David and Daniel – May 2005

The Home with No Boundaries

The third type of home with diminished order, structure, and routine is the home where no boundaries are set. In this home, there is not a set time for anything. There is no plan. There is no blue-print. These children live from car-to-car and house-to-house. In the home with no boundaries, children don't know when dinner is, if they are eating out again, or perhaps not eating at all.

Interestingly, as the children produced by the home with no boundaries get older they don't like to stay home. For example, they may like it at Grandmother's house where they sense safety, security, and some semblance of a routine. They know that they must do homework, bathe, and brush their teeth before bed. They also know that Granny makes them put all their things in the right place, and has a set time for bed.

When children who are raised in unstructured environments have structure applied later, they should not be allowed to rebel. Although children thrive in order, they will always choose the path of least resistance.

Children who are raised in unstructured homes will initially have issues in highly structured environments like school or church. In fact, most of the disagreements between parents and the adult caretakers of their children (whether in school, church, or elsewhere) is due to the caretaker insisting that a structure or a routine be followed with boundaries.

KEY DISCIPLE-MAKING POINTS

1. How early should boundaries be set in the lives of children?

   _____

   _____

   _____

2. What are some reasonable boundaries for children who are 2 to 4 years old?

   _____

   _____

   _____

3. Why is it important to establish boundaries early?

   _____

   _____

   _____

4. Do boundaries help establish parental authority? Why or why not?

   _____

   _____

   _____

5. What are some ways that parental authority can be established even when boundaries have not been previously set?

   _____

   _____

   _____

CHAPTER 7 – THE INTRODUCTION OF ORDER, STRUCTURE, AND DISCIPLINE

David and Daniel – 2007

"For whom the Lord loves, He corrects. Just as a father, the son in whom he delights." Proverbs 3:12

I have had very few children spend the night with my children over the years. The Bernard's are very structured, orderly people who insist that young children be trained.

Children who are not accustomed to training or being disciplined, resist it. Many parents do not parent their children at the level at which God has called Valerie and me to parent. The discipline and training that begins in the orderly, structured environment of the family home should extend to places away from home.

Children who are old enough to speak and understand are old enough to be trained and disciplined. This training should extend beyond the family home to other homes, restaurants, church, and school. It is important to demonstrate to children that good behavior is expected at all times in all places.

This is one of the great costs of parenting. Valerie and I spent many miserable evenings in restaurants with loud, and sometimes crying children. In those days, David and Daniel had to be trained in public places, like restaurants. On many of these occasions, Valerie and I spent more time talking and training them, than we spent addressing one another.

Sometimes home training doesn't travel well. For instance, I had a visiting child to defecate on the floor of our bathroom; right *next* to the toilet – instead of in the toilet. There was a whole group of children at our home that day, and I am sure they thought we would not be able to identify the perpetrator. But a part of establishing order is supervision.

We watched who was going in and out of the bathroom and we would go in each time after the children, to keep things in order. I could have identified the perpetrator, but I didn't. To do so would have been to risk dealing with parents who will support their child in almost anything – including wrong-doing.

I also had a child who played outside in the mud with my sons. When he came in to shower, he cleaned all the mud from his shoes with one of our bath towels. The mud was then washed down the sink.

Of course, it stopped up the sink. Again, I didn't mention it. If children are not raised in structured, orderly environments in the home, most likely they will not exhibit structure and order away from home. Accordingly, when those in authority attempt to apply structure, parents who are unaware of the importance of order and structure will usually uphold their children in wrongdoing.

David and Daniel are far from perfect. When they do get in trouble, because they do, all I ask is: "*Did you follow the rules?*" The rules are there to provide order, structure, and routine.

If our children know what the rules are, and they don't follow them, a corrective action plan must be put in place. Children should be taught that rules exist to help them understand the importance of order.

David – 2003

KEY DISCIPLE-MAKING POINTS

1. How early should parents establish rules or boundaries?

_____

_____

_____

2. What is the purpose of establishing rules/boundaries?

_____

_____

_____

3. How should parents respond when the rules are not followed or the boundaries are crossed?

_____

_____

_____

4. How important is it for parents to establish rules for places other than the family home?

_____

_____

_____

5. How should boundaries be set and enforced away from home?

_____

_____

_____

Daniel and David –2005

<u>God Reigns through Order</u>

God reigns through order. He is not the "*author of confusion*" (1ˢᵗ Corinthians 14:33). Chaos in the home indicates that boundaries have not been set or rules have not been enforced. God's plan for our lives continues unabated when peace has been brought about by order. God is glorified when there is peace.

Our actions should be reflective of the peace and order in our homes. Children who grow up in a home without order or routine, will naturally resist rules and disrupt the peace. When rules are resisted, the right of God to reign is resisted. A boy can't grow into a man of God without learning order.

Order begins very early with the establishment of physical routine - set times for feeding, changing, baths, and sleep. As mentioned in the previous chapter, these physical routines also foster a sense of psychological wellness and security. If this simple value (order, routine, discipline) is not learned as a first precept, intervention will be required later.

Years ago, boys were sent to the Army to become men. This was the intervention par excellence. What the Army taught men was that rules, routine, and order mattered if you were ever going to accomplish anything of worth. Likewise, if your children are going to grow up and accomplish anything of worth, they must first learn the lesson of order.

Ladies, if you are ever going to provide a home that is conducive to raising children of faith, there *must* be order and routine. When order and routine are established in the home, this orderliness will extend beyond the home into every situation in which children find themselves. The opposite is also true. There will be disorder and disharmony everywhere children go without order and routine in the family home.

Even as toddlers, David and Daniel would require food, prayer time and sleep at the same time each day, whether it was summer or fall and whether we were home or not. The routine became the routine and we all followed it.

One of my fondest memories of David as a three or four year-old is of him telling me when it was time to pray (*Daddy, let's pray*) and telling his brother when it was bed time (*Daniel, it's time for bed*). Years later, when Daniel was older and I was away from home on ministry business, Daniel would call at bedtime and want to know when was I coming home. He, like his brother, had become accustomed to the order and routine of our home.

This concept may be difficult to understand for some parents who have never experienced order and routine as children. There is safety and security where there is order. The safety and security that God gives to His children through order and routine follows them wherever they go in life. Some term this attribute "self-confidence." Others call it "self-esteem." Whatever it is, it is obvious when children have it and when they don't.

Safety and security, established by order and routine, should extend beyond the family home to the school, church, and elsewhere, so God can be glorified through your child in those places. After all, the decorum of our children is reflective of the condition of the homes in which they were raised.

David and Daniel fishing on Swan Lake

KEY DISCIPLE-MAKING POINTS

1. What is the best way to teach children order?

2. Does the level of cleanliness and general decorum in a home speak to the level of order that is present?

3. How does the outward appearance of children project the level of order present in the family home?

4. What are some of the benefits of children learning a routine?

5. What are some of the benefits of establishing order and routine in multiple settings?

David and Daniel – 2005

When Rules are Broken

There must be consequences when rules are broken. The Hebrew word for teaching and training are the same and it means to *"goad."* The goad is used to teach, but when the child crosses boundaries by disrupting the good order and peace of the home, it is also used as the rod of discipline.

In homes where order, structure, and discipline have been established, it is easy to spot when children are out of order or are resisting routine. There must be a remedy for children who resist routine.

For smaller children, discipline may be as simple as a parent saying *"no."* Every parent must learn to set boundaries early for acceptable and unacceptable behavior by saying *"no"* to some behaviors. *"No,"* can be said gently, even to toddlers.

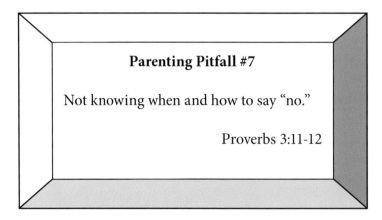

Parenting Pitfall #7

Not knowing when and how to say "no."

Proverbs 3:11-12

There can be no training, teaching, or discipline without correction. Love and correction go hand in hand. Without correction, parents can never assume the authority inherent in being a parent.

This is one of the first and most important lessons a parent will ever teach a child. A child's basic outlook on life is in his or her parents' hands. This very basic lesson of authority and accepting correction should be established early and often.

Those children who have not been corrected in the home never learn to accept responsibility for their actions. Later, they will argue with teachers, administrators, and anyone else in authority because their parents never assumed the authority inherent in parenting. This authority is made evident by the correction that occurs when rules are broken.

The failure of parents to administer correction hurts both the children, and later, the wider community in which they will live.

KEY DISCIPLE-MAKING POINTS

1. List some effective early forms of correction.

   _____

   _____

   _____

2. How does correction ensure that a parent will be viewed as a parent rather than as a friend or sibling?

   _____

   _____

   _____

3. Who is the first form of authority in a child's life?

   _____

   _____

   _____

   a. Why is this relationship significant?

      _____

      _____

      _____

   b. What are some possible consequences if this relationship is absent or unhealthy?

_____

_____

_____

4. How does establishing order, structure and discipline go hand in hand with correction?

_____

_____

_____

5. How do children benefit from correction?

_____

_____

_____

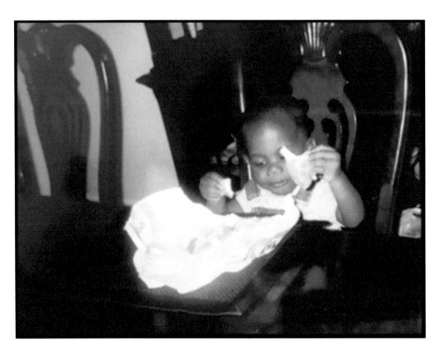

Daniel – 2004

CHAPTER 8 – GENDER DIFFERENTIATION

David – December 2000

"So God created man in his own image, in the image of God created he him; male and female created he them." Genesis 1:27 (KJV)

Years from now, if the Lord does not return beforehand, the entire Bible will be interpreted according to revisionist history. The term "Revisionist History" is a technical term. It means that history, or in this case Biblical history, will be re-interpreted to reflect the thoughts and sentiments of the age to come.

In the age to come, if you will allow me to go on record prophetically, it will be standard Biblical teaching that the first man, Adam, was a hermaphrodite. The thinking goes something like this: since Adam was perfect, fashioned at the hand of God and made in the image of God, then God Himself must be hermaphroditic in nature.

Thus the goal of men and women is to become such that both sexes are contained within each sex. To look at a man is to see a person so beautiful and perfect that he appears genderless. It also means to look at a woman and see a person who is so beautiful and so perfect, that she too appears genderless.

The prevailing thought of this still future age will be that names should not reflect gender. For example, "Pat" can either be 'Patrick' or 'Patricia' and "Sam" can either be 'Samuel' or 'Samantha.'

Clothes also will not reflect gender. More and more baby clothes are now gender neutral. Restroom accommodations also will not reflect gender. Any public restroom will be available to anyone at any-time, regardless of gender.

School textbooks will also not reflect gender. College applications, job applications and any forms where data is gathered, will not reflect gender. The historical precursors of this still-future age are being laid now in the form of same-sex marriage and what some call *"gender assignments."*

The term *"gender assignments"* is where people choose what gender they feel most comfortable with even though their "physical plumbing" would indicate something different. Those who believe themselves to be Christians and who practice *"gender assignment"* state plainly that *"God got their gender mixed up at birth."*

Now another historical precursor that is even more prevalent, but less likely to be noticed, is that of the masculine woman and the feminine man. In the age in which we now live, many women are more brash, assertive, loud, aggressive, and more likely to usurp masculine authority.

Indeed, we all must agree that this is the age where if a woman is going to be what we have historically described as "*feminine,*" she will be looked upon as "*helpless*" or "*weak.*"

Yes, this is the age of the masculine woman. The masculine woman is the precursor of the hermaphrodite. She is a woman biologically, but has the spiritual temperament of a man.

The exact opposite is true for men. Many men now are passive, docile, slow to take responsibility, slow to take the lead, and timid. This modern-day man is also the historical precursor to the still-future hermaphrodite. Now the Bible reads plainly in Genesis 1:27 that God created them *"male and female."*

The names of each sex indicated not only the gender, but the roles assigned to the gender. So when God created Adam, or the first man, manhood, or rather what it means to be a man, is set forth in him.

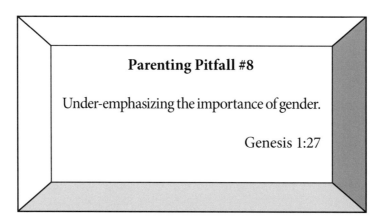

Parenting Pitfall #8

Under-emphasizing the importance of gender.

Genesis 1:27

One of the first things I taught my children – as early as their first year is that "*boys have penises and girls have vaginas.*" Crude yes, but perfect for one year-olds. I even drew pictures as the boys got older. Daniel reminds me of the picture I drew for him so long ago and David still tells his friends that his father taught him what a vagina is!

For my boys certain toys were off limits – such as dolls, kitchen supplies, sewing kits, and anything else that could be construed as being feminine.

If God would have blessed me with a girl also, my job of parenting as it pertains to gender would have been even more challenging. I would have been buying dolls, sewing kits, and kitchen supplies while also trying to keep David and Daniel away from the dolls, the sewing kits, and kitchen supplies. Yes, my sons do need to know their way around a kitchen and how to stitch, but early on, it was more important that they knew who God created them to be – gender included.

In fact, there must be a clear line drawn between children and the parents of the opposite sex. For example, David followed his mother everywhere she went as soon as he could crawl. If he couldn't go, he would whine and keep up a fuss. As this pertains to the bathroom, it created a problem. Read on.

When David graduated from high school, one day he confessed that he remembered some of the conversations about gender differentiation that we had when he was very young. As David and I talked, Daniel had to chime in as well about his earliest memories along those same lines. As usual, my younger son went into so much detail! I recorded him. This is what he said.

"Dad, when we were really young, you talked about private parts and which one's boys have and which one's girls have. You gave us examples by drawing them. Man, I can't believe you drew private parts like that! We were young but you were teaching us to act like men. You have always stressed responsibility and how to become a man."

"I remember you told me the story about how David used to urinate sitting down because he must have been in the restroom with Mom, so you had to teach him how to use the restroom like a boy should."

I think you get the idea. Parenting must reflect who God created the child to be, which includes gender. Parents are responsible for teaching children from an early age how to properly reflect their gender. While I am not a child psychologist, I would argue that this initial work in gender differentiation should be done prior to the completion of potty-training.

KEY DISCIPLE-MAKING POINTS

1. How early do you believe parents should stress gender?

_____

_____

_____

2. How can gender be stressed in the single parent home with a child of the opposite gender?

_____

_____

_____

3. How important is a parent's "modeling" of appropriate gender behavior?

_____

_____

_____

4. List some elements that may confuse young children about the importance of gender.

_____

_____

_____

5. How stringent should parents be in limiting their child's exposure to elements that may confuse them about gender?

_____

_____

_____

Daniel and David - 2007

CHAPTER 9 – O CHILD, WHERE ART THOU?

Daniel and David – 2004

*"If I ascend into heaven, You are there; If I make my bed in hell,
behold, You are there."* Psalm 139:8 (KJV)

In late 1999, Valerie and I purchased a home on a lake. In 2000, the same year David was born, she insisted that a fence be constructed between our home and the lake. Her fears were well founded – children can be tough to keep track of!

Some of the lessons of parenting are so basic that we are liable to miss them. As children become more mobile – crawling, scooting, and the various methods of travel that they employ, parental supervision becomes more important.

Sure, we applaud our children's independence, but that doesn't mean that they should be allowed to travel beyond the watchful eyes of parents. Although our children are in the same home, and perhaps just in the next room, parents are still responsible for knowing what small children are doing at all times.

This is the stage where the responsibility of parenting increases. There is not a time of the day or night that parents are not responsible for their pre-pubescent children. Most of the harm that children endure is due to the lack of parental oversight. This simple observation (no pun intended!) has kept children from much harm. Supervision is also a basic parental duty at which many parents fail because it is so costly to their personal freedom. Let me share with you two early examples from the same week in January of 2004.

"David is sleep. Daniel is crying. I've had the kids most of the day. Valerie got her hair done today. You know, I think I've had some bad assumptions about marriage and parenting. I viewed the children as being mostly Valerie's responsibility. But that's not true. I also put most of the housework on her or at least I have seen it as her responsibility. That's not true either."

"Valerie watches over the kids when I am at the Church and when they are sick. I guess that's a lot. She also stays busy with school. I've assumed that any woman who couldn't take care of the home and kids was a weakling, but school is tearing Valerie up. I've assumed correctly that I need to pull more weight. Right now she may be in a depression. Neither of us knew it would be this hard." Midnight, Friday, January 2, 2004.

You know, if I had really known the level of responsibility required to parent children, I probably would have agreed with Valerie and not had any! This was a tough week coming out of the holidays – which meant extra services at the Church I served.

Each time we attended service it seemed that we had to pack up the entire house and circle back a couple of times when we remembered what we had left behind. Then too, it was really cold which made our tasks even more cumbersome.

David and Daniel were both walking – twin terrors! They were into everything. The more they moved, the closer we had to watch them. We had agreed early on that we would be responsible for the care of our children – not their grandmothers, other family members, or friends. Consider the following journal entry from just two weeks later.

"The last week and a half has been tough. Daniel was sick – high fever, cough, irritable and the doctor put him on flu medication. I stayed home with him for a week. Sister Reginal [Valerie's mother] was not feeling well herself, although she had not kept the children for a couple of weeks. I think she is really tired and didn't put up much of a fuss when we said that we would put Daniel in the daycare center with David to give her some rest."

"This week, David got sick and Daniel got better. David is not coughing but he has had high temps –in the range of 104. The doctor said 'virus' but he also complains about his teeth hurting. The result is that I have been unable to be 'free' during the day to spend extended time in prayer and calling on members. Valerie is irked because she stays stressed with our children. I have been accepted to Wesley Seminary, which means more work, more study, and more money spent." 7:01 am Wednesday, January 14, 2004

I soon learned that the responsibility of children was not an interruption to my otherwise idyllic life, the responsibility of children became my life. As the children grew from infants to toddlers, we had even more to learn about parenting. Our sons could not be left alone for any appreciable period of time. They were not only a danger to themselves, but to everything we owned!

"I kept David and Daniel for 5+ hours in the early afternoon and evening. David sure knows how to make me mad by yelling, hitting Daniel, destroying photo albums, books and everything else." 11 pm Saturday, January 3, 2004

Valerie and I knew that whenever we could not hear the children it was bad news if we were not in the same room with them. So that is what we started to do – remain in the room with our children – especially if they were going to be a while. If there was some sort of accident, Valerie and I would always ask one another *"where were you?"* or *"why weren't you watching?"*

This parenting technique proved fortuitous because we quickly learned how dangerous a "normal" house can be to small children. Additionally, most everything we had in the house could be detrimental to the health of one or both of our children.

And it was a real sacrifice to make sure that each child was properly supervised. This usually meant that we could not multi-task. When the children were home and we were responsible for watching them, that is usually all we could do.

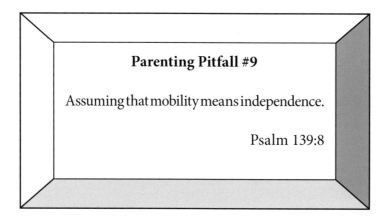

Parenting Pitfall #9

Assuming that mobility means independence.

Psalm 139:8

It was tough getting used to the fact that you could not devote yourself to anything else that required most of your attention when the children were home. You had to be present with them, in the moment.

For Valerie, her natural, nurturing motherly instincts served her well. For a busy Pastor, I got a first-class lesson on patience. My children not only needed my attention, by their actions they demanded it. There were times when I felt guilty that they were in daycare, but the Lord knew that Valerie and I needed the rest as well as the separation.

Up to this point, most things in our marriage had been mundane and "ho-hum," but the older the children got, the more they required our active planning and oversight. For instance, they could not go in public restrooms unless I went in with them. As they got older, one could not go without the other. There had to be supervision. They also could not be left alone with teenagers – family or not – not even for a moment.

As a Pastor, I had heard enough horror stories about the prolonged sexual abuse of one child by an older child or by a person who was "baby-sitting" or in some other position of authority.

Valerie and I even agreed that we would not put our sons in any form of childcare outside of the home until they were confident enough to talk and tell Mommy and Daddy about their day. Our sons also took the teachings of our home with them as protection.

KEY DISCIPLE-MAKING POINTS

1. Why is the supervision of small children so important?

_____

_____

_____

2. Do you believe that small children should be allowed some time away from their parents during the day?

_____

_____

_____

3. With all of the time that we spend with our children supervising them, what is one of the by-products?

_____

_____

_____

4. How does having a parent nearby increase the confidence and self-esteem of small children?

_____

_____

_____

5. What are some ways that single parents of multiple children can adequately supervise them?

_____

_____

_____

Daniel and David – 2004

CHAPTER 10 – HOW CAN I PROTECT MY CHILD?

David, Reginald, and Daniel – June 2011

"Repeat them again and again to your children. Talk about them when you are at home and when you are on the road, when you are going to bed and when you are getting up." Deuteronomy 6:7 (KJV)

"How can I protect my child?" is one of the more basic questions of parenthood. With all the dangers of the modern world – bullying, cyber stalking, sexual predators, and identity theft just to name a few – there is a need for increased safety and security for our children.

Sadly, the more of an unfriendly place the world has become, the less adept parents have become in protecting their children from this world.

Our 21st century world has become more complex in its assaults against our Christian sensibilities, but our parenting skills have not risen to the occasion. We behave as if the best way to keep our children safe is to keep them at home.

This may work for a small child, but it also has the unintended effect of making him or her never want to leave home. Young adults are staying home longer than ever and working less than ever.

When our children leave home, they often find that they are ill-prepared to deal with the onslaught of false information, sinful situations, and downright deceitful and even racist people.

This is the failure par excellence of proper parenting. Parenting should prepare children for what they will face in the world at large when they leave home. I like to call this form of parental instruction, "finishing school." Before I explain what this most effective tool is, let me explain what it isn't.

The most effective tool that God gives parents in protecting their children is not something physical – like locks and bolts. This tool is also not financial. Money is good, and you need money if you plan to keep a roof over your head and food on your table, but a 16ᵗʰ century English poet stated that *"a fool and his money are soon parted."*

The emotional aspects of parenting, such as unconditional love and acceptance, are absolutely wonderful and also essential, but if love alone could protect our children, none of them would ever get hurt.

The Word of God provides the only remedy for how to protect our children and it can be summed up in one word: teaching. Parents should beware of the psychological phenomenon that some have termed the "parental guilt trap." All of us parents have been in this trap or will be in it.

It is the emotion that you feel when something bad happens to your child and you wonder what you could have done to protect them from it. It is when you bash yourself over the job you did in preparing them to face the world.

If you want to avoid the parental guilt trap, or at least mitigate its effect, you must put your children in the position to hear some solid Biblical teaching.

The answer to protecting your children is not in name brand clothes. The answer is not even in the schools that they attend. The answer is not in any club or group that they could ever join. The answer is this: what are they being taught from the Word of God?

Parents can't always be with their children, but their *teaching* can. The teaching that parents instill in their children, for better or worse, goes where the children go. Even when children no longer have access to their parents – the parent's values are still present because of the teaching they instilled.

KEY DISCIPLE-MAKING POINTS

1. What are some ways that you want to protect your child?

_____

_____

_____

2. What is your plan to accomplish protecting your child?

_____

_____

_____

3. As a parent, what values do you believe are important for your child to possess?

_____

_____

_____

4. How do you plan to instill these values in your child?

_____

_____

_____

5. How do you plan to prepare your child for the time when they will no longer have continuous access to you?

_____

_____

_____

David - 2007

Teaching Forms a Barrier

The appropriate time for teaching your children is while they are in your home with no distractions. This teaching should begin as soon as possible preparing them for what is ahead.

The content of the teaching should be based on your past – what *you* experienced and witnessed as a child their age, but also their future, what they can expect to face in the months and years ahead.

Since we want to protect our children, we have to provide them teaching about their future that separates them from other children who don't share their values. That's right. This is the heart of Christianity – possessing Christian values that endure.

For example, in the Old Testament it was the Law of Moses that gave the Israelites their distinctiveness. Moses put it this way in Deuteronomy 4:8: "*And what great nation has decrees and regulations as righteous and fair as this body of instructions that I am giving you today?*" (NLT)

Likewise, parents should have a long list of do's and don'ts – a body of regulations and decrees. Jehovah had a list for the Children of Israel, and He commanded that these do's and don'ts be taught to the children by their parents.

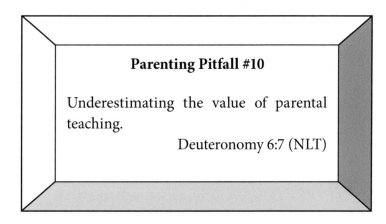

Parenting Pitfall #10

Underestimating the value of parental teaching.

Deuteronomy 6:7 (NLT)

When children are consistently taught the Biblical, moral, and spiritual do's and don'ts appropriate for their age, it creates a spiritual barrier around them.

Moses implored the Children of Israel in Deuteronomy 6:7: "*Repeat them again and again to your children. Talk about them when you are at home and when you are on the road, when you are going to bed and when you are getting up.*" I know this sounds hard but it's not. It's actually quite simple.

When David and Daniel were in the range of four to six years old, I used the time that we spent in the vehicle to talk to them about such things as good touch/bad touch; who you can talk to, who you shouldn't talk to; who you can leave with and who you can't leave with, etc.

That was a lot of time spent talking. As they got older, I dedicated one meal a week to be a teaching meal – usually lunch on Saturdays. Over lunch, my wife and I talked to them about the do's and the don'ts appropriate for their age. Over time this teaching created a spiritual barrier between them and others.

This barrier gives children a sense of worth and uniqueness in the world, as they begin to understand that there are other people who don't share their values, or rather who don't have this barrier of teaching around them. Moses put the same idea this way in Deuteronomy 4:6:

"*Keep them* [these regulations] *faithfully because that will show your wisdom and insight to the nations who will hear about all these regulations. They will say, 'Surely this great nation is a wise and insightful people!'*" (NLT)

You don't have to tell your children that they are special; if you teach them well enough at home, they will see the difference between themselves and others when they attend daycare; when they start school, and even when they are at church. This teaching is precisely what will protect your child when you are not around.

They will understand that there are some people that they should not let behind this barrier or let have undue influence over them. To continue with my Old Testament example, Moses taught the Children of Israel because there needed to be a barrier between them and the Canaanites.

Ethnically, the ancient Jews were very similar to the Moabites, the Edomites and the other inhabitants of Canaan. The major difference is in the values that they held.

Likewise, parental teaching transmits values to children which will identify who is healthy enough for them to associate with and who is not.

Teaching will identify those values (practices) that are acceptable and those values (practices) that are not acceptable.

KEY DISCIPLE-MAKING POINTS

1. When do you teach your children?

_____

_____

_____

2. Why is constant teaching so important?

_____

_____

_____

3. Why is teaching our children how to make discriminating judgments of character important?

_____

_____

_____

4. How might the values we transmit to our children reinforce their value and worth as individuals?

_____

_____

_____

5. How might the lack of teaching values affect a child's safety in this world?

_____

_____

_____

David and Daniel - 2014

Teaching Forms a Buttress

A buttress, used in this sense, is something that identifies a falsehood. Our children live in a world of ideas. Some of these ideas are good. Others are not so good. Parents are responsible for protecting the young, impressionable minds of their children.

An unhappy, unhealthy, unfriendly person doesn't have to come to your home or even to your child's school to get in their heads and expose them to unhealthy ideas.

If your child has access to an iPhone or a computer, he or she is exposed to all kinds of ideas. If you don't have a buttress in your child's head, you can't protect them from any of it.

Teaching Biblical ideas and a Biblical worldview to your child forms a mental buttress that will resist any worldly ideas and worldly temptations.

Parents can't fight what is in their child's mind unless some healthy teaching is placed there prior to anything else. A buttress is something that supports or strengthens something else.

Teaching your children how to observe the world through a Biblical worldview will train their young minds to reject anything that is not consistent with what God has said. Children will find themselves in a lot of trouble if they don't learn how to function in a world of ideas.

They must know how to reject the very idea of something. This lesson must be taught as soon as possible if the child is going to survive the onslaught of hormones associated with puberty.

David, now a college student, is always on some sort of group project where ideas have to be debated. He knows immediately that if God has spoken against it, he can't be for it, and even more importantly, if God has spoken against it, it can't be good for anybody.

This is the buttress that is needed in a world where somebody is always trying to deceive somebody else – even through lifestyles presented in textbooks and glorified on television, social media, and school campuses.

To pick up my Old Testament example again, Moses warned the Children of Israel about the Canaanites they would encounter, but he also explained why these people had to be driven from the Promised Land.

Moses explained it by getting them to understand complex ideas like idolatry. This firm teaching on idolatry would become a buttress, or layer of protection, in the Promised Land.

Firm teaching keeps Christians from falling for any *"wooden nickels,"* or any *"fake dimes."* This buttress goes places that mother and father can't go. This type of teaching helps the child discern between good and evil.

The Word of God is knowledge. It is a *"lamp unto our feet"* and a *"light unto our path."* To have it, is to know what something is, not through experience, but because of what God has said about it. So when an idea is pitched to your child, he or she has a light that they can hold up to it and examine it.

David and Daniel's childhood home, Swan Lake, Jackson, Mississippi

KEY DISCIPLE-MAKING POINTS

1. Have you taught your child what God has said about sin?

    _____

    _____

    _____

2. How have you taught your child to say "no" to some things?

    _____

    _____

    _____

3. Has your child witnessed you refuse some things on moral grounds?

    _____

    _____

    _____

4. Have you taught your child how to make good decisions based on the merits of an idea?

    _____

    _____

    _____

5. How can the omnipresence of God be an effective teaching tool for good decision-making?

    _____

    _____

    _____

Daniel and David - 2017

Teaching Forms a Belief System

What you present as true to your child, if presented early and often enough, will be accepted as truth. Everybody believes something. Our belief systems form the core of who we are.

If our children see us living any kind of way when they are young, they will catch on to the unspoken beliefs inherent in a loose lifestyle. The lifestyle of the parent, while the child is not yet school age, is the greatest teacher of all. To pick up our Old Testament example one more time, this is the very reason why Moses was not going to make it to the Promised Land.

He was told in Numbers 20:8 to speak to the rock while the congregation of Israel looked on. Instead, Moses got angry and struck the rock. The Children of Israel witnessed it all. The Lord told Moses in verse 12, "*You didn't trust me.*" (NLT)

You can protect your children by letting them see you trust God. If they see you trust God early and often enough, it will give them something to believe in.

Children who are 5 or 6 years old know whether their parents pray or not. They also know how important Church attendance is. Children learn the value of the Word of God when they see it read over and over. This pattern put before them becomes the standard by which they measure themselves.

It pleases this Pastor's heart to see Daniel read and study from a Bible that I purchased for his mother three years before he was born. Year after year as a child, he witnessed his mother reading that particular Bible.

Daniel also requested the Bible of his maternal grandmother, Corine Reginal, upon her death. He reads from it as well. When I see the Christian values that have been developed in him, I am reminded of what Paul told Timothy in 2nd Timothy 1:5: "*I remember your genuine faith, for you share the faith that first filled your grandmother Lois and your mother, Eunice. And I know that same faith continues strong in you.*" (NLT)

Children want to believe. They are given the mindset to believe. They just need their parents to teach them to believe. By doing so, they will be protected for an eternity.

KEY DISCIPLE-MAKING POINTS

1. Are there Bibles visible in your home?

_____

_____

_____

2. Does your child witness you reading the Bible?

_____

_____

_____

3. Do you take your child to Church?

_____

_____

_____

4. Do you engage your child in everyday talk about God?

_____

_____

_____

5. Do you teach your child, by example, to pray in situations that he or she cannot control?

_____

_____

_____

MY CHILD, MY DISCIPLE

Pastoral Reflections on Parenting

David, Valerie, Reginald and Daniel – 2017

"As for me and my house, we will serve the Lord." Joshua 24:15 (KJV)

Postlude

The word "postlude" is a musical term. It indicates a musical selection or medley of selections that are played following a religious program. The postlude provides some "parting thoughts" so to speak.

More and more parents only begin to parent during the preteen and teenage years when the foundation for parenting should have already been set from the very beginning.

Pastoral Reflections on Parenting focuses on the early years of a child's life and even the choices the child's parents made prior to the birth of the child.

Some view this time period as not being as significant from a parenting perspective as the preteen and teenage years. From this pastor's perspective, the exact opposite is true.

Parenting begins "at the beginning," which is dating. After all, first things must be first (Chapter 1 – "First Things First"). Dating should be with the intention of Christian marriage (Chapter 2 – "The Purpose of Godly Dating").

If it is the Lord's will, there will be "A Christian Marriage" (Chapter 3) leading to a pregnancy (Chapter 4 – "Conception to Birth"). From there, the training wheels come off (Chapter 5 – *"A Real, Live Birth!"*) and the fun begins (Chapter 6 – *"Let the Training Begin!"*).

Our parenting skills are further honed as we introduce "Order, Structure, and Discipline" (Chapter 7) as well as "Gender Differentiation" (Chapter 8). Our foundational work as parents is practically done as we provide supervision (Chapter 9 – "O Child, Where Art Thou?") and consider "How Can I Protect My Child?" (Chapter 10).

From here, I leave the work for the foundation has been set. Each builder (parent) is called to build on it. Paul put the same thought this way in 1st Corinthians 3:10-11: *"Because of God's grace to me, I have laid the foundation like an expert builder. Now others are building on it. But whoever is building on this foundation must be very careful. For no one can lay any foundation other than the one we already have— Jesus Christ." (NLT)*

Daniel and David – October 2003

Printed in the United States
By Bookmasters